MARÍA GÓMEZ LARA (Bogotá, 1989) has published the poetry collections *Después del horizonte (After the Horizon)* (2012), *Contratono (Countertone)* (Visor, 2015), *El lugar de las palabras (The Place Where Words Reside)* (Pre-Textos, 2020), *Don Quijote a voces (Don Quixote out loud)* (Pre-Textos, 2024) and the anthology *Palabras piel (Skin Words)* (Frailejón Editores, 2022). *Contratono* won the XXVII Loewe Foundation International Poetry Prize for Emerging Writers and includes a prologue by the Uruguayan poet Ida Vitale. It was also translated into Portuguese by the poet Nuno Júdice under the title Nó de sombras (2015). Some of her poems have also been translated into Italian, English, Chinese and Arabic and have appeared, both in Spanish and in bilingual editions, in different media in Latin America and Spain and in numerous anthologies of Colombian and Latin American poetry. She studied literature at the Universidad de los Andes in Bogotá, holds an M.F.A. in creative writing in Spanish from New York University and an M.A. in Romance literatures and languages from Harvard University, where she also earned a PhD in Latin American poetry. She is currently a professor at Tufts University in Madrid.

CURTIS BAUER is a poet and translator from the United States. His most recent poetry collection is American Selfie (Barrow Street Press, 2019). He lives in Spain and Texas and teaches creative writing and comparative literature at Texas Tech University.

The Place Where Words Reside

First edition: October, 2025
Original Title: El lugar de las palabras

© María Gómez Lara, 2020
Published by agreement with Pre-textos S.L.U
© of the translation Curtis Bauer, 2025
All rights reserved. Published in the United States of America
by Broken Bowl Books

Manufactured in the United States of America
Cover engraving: Víctor Ramírez

Broken Bowl Books
PO BOX 450948
Laredo TX 78045-0023
www.brokenbowlbooks.com

Total or partial reproduction of this work, by any means or process whatsoever, is strictly forbidden without the written authorization of the copyright holders under the sanctions established by the law.

ISBN: 978-1-969317-13-2
Library of Congress Control Number: 2025947663

María Gómez Lara
The Place Where Words Reside

Translated by Curtis Bauer

Broken Bowl / Books

Recuerdo, déjenme recordar
(tengo que asirme de algo hasta que se atavíe de color lo invisible),
entre la incertidumbre y el pavor recuerdo cualquier día,
cuando el mundo empezaba frente a mis pies menudos como un festival de soles
invitándome a entrar,
y yo con los bolsillos repletos de cristales, de cosechas sagradas y amuletos

Olga Orozco,
«*Algunas anotaciones alrededor del miedo*»

I remember, let me remember
(I have to hold on to something until the invisible is dressed in color).

between the uncertainty and dread I remember any given day,
when the world began in front of my tiny feet like a festival of suns
inviting me to enter,
and me with my pockets full of crystals, sacred crops and amulets

OLGA OROZCO,

"A Few Annotations About Fear"

Índice / Contents

11   *Preface*

12   I Para cubrirme la voz / *I How to shelter my voice*
Mi primer poema cardiocéntrico   14
My First Cardiocentric Poem   15
Un abrigo de invierno   24
A Winter Coat   25
Debí alejarme silbando   28
I Should Have Walked Away Whistling   29
Brain tumor unit   34
Brain Tumor Unit   35
El cerebro no duele   38
The Brain Feels No Pain   39

42   II Nombrar una herida en las palabras / *II To Name a Wound Inside My Words*
Nombrar una herida en las palabras   44
To Name a Wound Inside My Words   45
Decir tengo miedo   60
To Say I Am Scared   61
El lugar de las palabras   64
The Place Where Words Reside   65
A un centímetro   76
Within One Centimeter   77

82   III Lo que pase cuando corten mi materia / *III What Will Happen When My Matter Is Cut Away*
Una cicatriz   84
A Scar   85
Para un cuerpo que está solo   94
For a Body That Is Alone   95
Tengo miedo del túnel   102
I Am Scared Of The Tunnel   103

108 IV Cómo me cosí esa cicatriz / *IV How I Stitched Up That Scar*
Ese sonido   106
That Sound   *107*
Un examen de rutina   110
A Routine Examination   *111*
Escóndete en tu abrigo   118
Hide Inside Your Coat   *119*
Palabras piel   132
Skin Words   *133*
Frida Kahlo   134
Frida Kahlo   *135*

149   *Translator's Note*

Preface

These days, poetry books tend to be collections of verses written by the author over a period of time. Sometimes, and it doesn't matter, they have no thematic unity, brought together by the common denominator of a single author. Poetry books with a thematic unity are more scarce. And even more scarce still are those that tell a story from the first page to the last: this is the case of *El lugar de las palabras* (The Place Where Words Reside) and the story it tells happened to the author herself, María Gómez Lara (Bogotá, 1989). One fine day, "on the screen, an X-ray of your brain / they show you a perfectly defined heart-shaped stain / an indeterminate lesion in the left frontal lobe / the neurologists don't recognize it / possible low-grade tumor / and the world suddenly falls to the floor, you collapse."

The story told in *El lugar de las palabras* begins there. It continues with "hospital needles, my arms battered / they can't find my veins anymore." The doctor reassures her ("there's no need to worry, you'll recover") and also distresses her ("There's a chance / that you might lose / your words"). The fear of losing words: "... my words / I never thought they were / in danger / that one day I might / not find them / words always came / to rescue me." "I'm so scared / I don't know where to put it." Then, after tests and more tests, the doctors decide on surgery to remove the heart-shaped spot: "they're going to open my brain to take out my heart."

No; true to the law of Gozar Leyendo, I'm not going to tell you the ending, but I will say that it's a shocking book. There is an overwhelming, profound, unabashed sincerity here. An overflowing sincerity that is nevertheless expressed in controlled language, with great craft, a lot of literary work and so much poetic wisdom that the words flow like poems and intimate confessions at the same time. Moving and excellent.

Darío Jaramillo Agudelo

I

Para cubrirme la voz

I

How To Shelter My Voice

Mi primer poema cardiocéntrico

I

la palabra corazón no aparece nunca en sus poemas dijo un poeta y
 amigo muy generoso para elogiarme
ella expresa el dolor con la ruptura de las partes duras los huesos
 las rodillas los codos y *su envoltura la piel*

pues aquí va
mi primer poema cardiocéntrico:

en la pantalla una radiografía de tu cerebro

te muestran una mancha en forma de corazón perfecto
 bien delimitado
lesión indeterminada en el lóbulo frontal izquierdo
los neurólogos no la reconocen
posible tumor de bajo grado
y el mundo se te cae al suelo de repente te desplomas
no puede ser cierta esta pesadilla oí mal que por favor ya me despierte

tengo algo en el cerebro

parece un mal chiste de la vida
ahora sí
se le fue la mano en la ironía
y eso que ya hace años
aprendiste a reírte de tristeza

pero tanto sufrir por amor
tanto que no te quisieron

My First Cardiocentric Poem

I

the word heart never appears in her poems a generous poet and
    friend said in praise of my work
she expresses pain through the breakage of the hard parts the
    bones the knees the elbows and their covering the skin

so here it goes
my first cardiocentric poem:

on the screen an x-ray of your brain

they show you a perfect heart-shaped spot
    well-defined
indeterminate lesion on the left frontal lobe
the neurologists do not recognize it
a possible low-grade tumor
and the world comes crashing down around you you collapse
this nightmare can't be true i heard wrong please wake me up now

i have something in my brain

it seems like one of life's bad jokes
this is it
the irony is too much
and now it's been years since
you learned to laugh out of sadness

but so much suffering for love
so much that they didn't love you

tanta soledad
tanto amor que ocupaba el hueco completo de su ausencia

tú que conociste todas las formas de lo que no es amor

viste tantas sutilezas de la pena
que lo que nunca hiciste
fue dibujar corazones

nadie te dio nunca
una caja de chocolates en forma de corazón
con corazoncitos de chocolate adentro
ni bombas ni confetis de corazones
nadie te dio nunca un ramo de rosas rojas
con un moño gigante y una tarjeta estampada de corazones
todos los san valentín los pasaste en tu casa en pijama
y declarabas toque de queda
para estar tranquila
para que no te pusieran un corazón de crema en el café
para que no te restregaran en la cara el amor ajeno

nadie te dijo te amo
porque sólo supieron no quererte
cada uno a su manera
cada uno con su herida
cada uno fue dejándote
su propia cicatriz irrepetible

so much loneliness
so much love that it filled the entire void of its absence

you who knew all the forms of what is not love

you saw so many subtleties of grief
what you never did
was draw hearts

no one ever gave you
a heart-shaped box of chocolates
with little chocolate hearts inside
no fireworks no heart-shaped confetti
no one ever gave you a bouquet of red roses
with a giant bow and a card printed with hearts
you spent every valentine's day at home in your pajamas
and you imposed a curfew on yourself
to be calm
so they wouldn't pour a heart of cream onto your coffee
so they wouldn't rub other people's love in your face

no one told you i love you
because they only knew not to love you
each in his own way
each with a unique wound
each was leaving you
his own unrepeatable scar

II

por eso lo tuyo fue el cerebro

lo tuyo fue pensar
repetirte una y otra vez voy a estar bien
a esta sobrevivo
peores golpes me han dado

por eso

aprendiste pronto a razonar
a recurrir a la lógica
aunque no tenga sentido nada
puedo llorar llorar acoplar la fuerza
decirle a mi cerebro que me salve:

que piense cosas para sostenerme a flote

cosas por ejemplo
esto no es contra ti
y ya pudiste rearmarte muchas veces
por ejemplo tú eres fuerte
y no hay confabulaciones de los astros
sino una racha de mala suerte
(inexplicable) (inagotable) (eterna)

pero explícala

búscale por dónde
(dicen que la imaginación también está en el cerebro)
invéntale algún orden

II

that's why your thing was the brain

your thing was to think
repeat over and over again i'll be fine
i'll survive this
i've been dealt worse blows

that's why

you learned to reason early
to turn to logic
even if it makes no sense at all
i can cry cry gather my strength
tell my brain to save me:

to think of things to keep me from drowning

things like
this is not about you
and you've already put yourself back together so many times
for example you are strong
and the stars are not aligned against you
but this is a streak of bad luck
(inexplicable) (inexhaustible) (eternal)

but explain it

look for a way
(they say that imagination is also inside the brain)
come up with some order

lo tuyo fue salvarte con palabras

entonces habla
dile a tu cerebro   repítele repítele
que por favor no se enferme
en forma de corazón

que mucho he sobrevivido

para que ahora me enferme
de todo el amor que no tuve

de tanto que pensé
para salvarme

para que ahora me muestren
esta imagen

del corazón desafiante
burlándose de mí

your thing was to save yourself with words

then speak
tell your brain   repeat it repeat it
please don't get sick
heart-shaped

i have survived so much

so that now i get sick
from all the love i never had

so much i thought
to save myself

so that now they show me
this image

of a defiant heart
mocking me

III

agujas hospitales los brazos maltratados
ya no me encuentran las venas
me conectan electrodos tengo miedo

tal vez de tanto dolor

de pensar para no sentir
acabé sintiendo hasta la médula
hasta que mi pobre corazón herido
se me escondió en la cabeza

para cubrirse del derrumbe
para esquivar las flechas
para creerse a salvo

para darse por un rato
una tregua una trinchera

III

hospital needles battered arms
they can no longer find my veins
they connect electrodes to me i am scared

perhaps from so much pain

to think so i do not feel
i felt it in my marrow
until my poor wounded heart
hid in my head

huddled against the collapse
to dodge the arrows
to believe it was safe

to take a break for a while
a truce a trench

Un abrigo de invierno

Para mi mamá
que se empeña en regalarme abrigos de invierno

mi primer reflejo

después de escribir
dos poemas
fue comprar un abrigo de invierno

como si fuera lo más urgente   al recibir la noticia:

primera prioridad de acción
para no quedarme

estancada

congelada de la angustia
empecé a investigar

quería un abrigo de una marca canadiense
de esos que se usan en el polo
para inviernos que nunca sospeché
inviernos peores que este

quería un abrigo de un color brillante
vi uno rojo encendido y me encantó
un abrigo para no perderme en la nieve
un abrigo para recordarme aquí estoy yo
aquí estoy yo con mis colores no me he ido

quería algo concreto para resguardarme
algo para tocar

A Winter Coat

For my mamá
who insists on giving me winter coats

my first reflex

after writing
two poems
was to buy a winter coat

as if it were the most urgent thing to do   when i received the news:

first priority
so i do not get

stuck

frozen with anguish
i did my research

i wanted a canadian brand coat
one of those used on the north pole
for the winters i never imagined
winters worse than this one

i wanted a brightly colored coat
i saw a fiery red one i loved
a coat so i won't get lost in the snow
a coat to remind me i am here
i am here with my colors i haven't gone away

i wanted something tangible to protect me
something to touch

un escudo una armadura un amuleto

pero si tienes tantos abrigos
no necesitas otro

necesito ese

porque todos los que tengo son insuficientes
porque el invierno que se viene
no habría podido imaginarlo

porque quiero protegerme de algo   cualquier cosa:

protegerme del frío
proteger mi piel contra la nieve
aunque sea inútil

aunque mi cuerpo esté solo

aunque no tenga cómo
abrigarme del miedo

aunque no pueda   hacer nada

para ampararme el cerebro
para envolver la conciencia
para cubrirme la voz

a shield a suit of armor an amulet

but if you already have so many coats
you don't need another one

i need this one

because all the ones i have are not enough
because of the winter that's coming
i couldn't have imagined it

because i want to protect myself from something   from anything:

protect myself from the cold
protect my skin from the snow
even if it's useless

even if my body is alone

even if i don't have a way
to blanket myself from fear

even if i cannot   do anything

to shield my brain
to envelop my conscience
to shelter my voice

Debí alejarme silbando

> *Me alejo silbando del molino, silbando*
> *para disimular*
> *el temor de poner el pie*
> *en una huella sin esperanza*
> José Watanabe, "El miedo"

debí alejarme silbando

aunque no sepa silbar
debí alejarme corriendo cojeando balbuceando
debí alejarme de alguna forma debí alejarme
    como fuera
debí alejarme cantando *vete de mí* y nunca vuelvas

debí haber oído el estruendo

de tu huella sin esperanza
debí haber sentido en la espalda
el frío de tu fuga
anunciándome el peligro desde antes

pero esta vez no dudé

aún no entiendo por qué
no vi o no pude ver

me puse una venda en los ojos
me quité las gafas a propósito
me quité las gafas porque quise

y cuando vi tu huella borrosa apenas dibujada

I Should Have Walked Away Whistling

> *I walk away from the mill whistling, whistling*
> *to conceal*
> *the fear of stepping*
> *into a hopeless footprint*
> JOSÉ WATANABE, "FEAR"

i should have walked away whistling

even if i don't know how to whistle
i should have moved away running limping stammering
i should have walked away somehow i should have walked away
    no matter what
i should have walked away singing *vete de mí* and never come back

i should have heard the rumble

of your hopeless footprint
i should have felt the chill
of your escape on my back
warning me of the danger to come

but this time i didn't hesitate

i still don't know why
i didn't see or couldn't see

i tied a blindfold over my eyes
i deliberately took off my glasses
i took off my glasses because i wanted to

and when i saw your blurred footprint barely drawn

me dije al fin encontraste una trinchera
para cubrirte del desastre

vi tu huella en el suelo
y sin pensarlo dos veces

en vez de alejarme silbando la pisé

cuando pisé tu huella sin esperanza
quedé aturdida
me explotó en el pie de repente   su vacío

ahora cómo huyo de ti
ahora dónde me escondo de tu sombra
ahora con qué palabras

le explico
a mi pie herido
que se apure
(debí alejarme cojeando)

porque el fondo de tu huella estaba hueco

era una huella sin pie
sin pasado de presencia
era el rastro de tanto que no estuvo
una trampa disfrazada de espejismo
debí creerle al miedo

(al miedo que no tuve a tiempo al que esta vez me faltó
al miedo
que estaba ahí haciendo señas saltando pero por qué no quise
    verlo y fui quitándome las gafas)

i told myself you finally found a trench
to shield you from disaster

i saw your footprint on the ground
and without a second thought

instead of walking away whistling i stepped on it

when i stepped into your hopeless footprint
i was stunned
its emptiness suddenly exploded into   my foot

now how do i get away from you
now where can i hide from your shadow
now with what words

can i explain
to my wounded foot
it needs to hurry
(i should have limped away)

because the bottom of your footprint was hollow

it was a footprint without a foot
without presence in its past
it was the trace of so much not there
a trap disguised as a mirage
i should have believed in fear

(the fear i didn't have in time that this time i was lacking
fear
that was there waving and jumping around but why didn't i want
    to see it and i was taking off my glasses)

debí creerle al miedo
de tu huella sin esperanza

una huella
que bien habría podido

ser tierra seca erosionada

i should have believed in the fear
of your hopeless footprint

a footprint
that could well have been

eroded dry land

Brain tumor unit

brain tumor unit dice una grabación al otro lado de la línea
deje un mensaje y la secretaria de la secretaria del doctor
puede que algún día le devuelva la llamada

brain tumor unit
parece mentira pero es cierto no me equivoqué
es el número correcto
ya he llamado diez veces   siguen sin darme la cita

brain tumor unit

tal vez   si dejo de llamar
desaparezca esto y se borre todo   de repente

podría
colgar el teléfono
hacer como si nada   olvidar   podría olvidar

recuperarme rescatar   mi vida   aunque sea   a las malas

podría pedirle a mi cerebro que se cure
o cubrir
con un grito
el miedo silenciar el qué tal si

para ocuparme otra vez de los desastres cotidianos:

el desamor
la soledad
la confusión
la rabia la rabia

Brain Tumor Unit

brain tumor unit a recording says on the other end of the line
i leave a message and the secretary of the doctor's secretary
might one day return your call

brain tumor unit
it's hard to believe but it's true i was not wrong
it is the correct number
i've already called ten times   i still haven't been given an appointment

brain tumor unit

maybe   if i stop calling
it all goes away and everything is erased   suddenly

i could
hang up the telephone
pretend as if nothing   forget   i could forget

recover rescue   my life   even if   out of nowhere   the pain

i could ask my brain to heal
or hide
with a scream
the fear to silence the what if

again deal with everyday disasters:

heartbreak
loneliness
confusion
the rage the rage

la angustia
la tristeza
la clase que voy a dar mañana
la ropa para lavar acumulada
los platos apilados en la cocina

todo menos esto
todo menos oír una vez más
brain tumor unit

brain tumor unit
llamo otra vez
espero
en la línea
qué más da qué puedo hacer

brain tumor unit
dejo otro mensaje
a ver si esta es la vencida

me trago el miedo   invento   alguna fuerza

otra vez
vuelvo a empezar

the anguish
sadness
the class i'm going to teach tomorrow
the mound of laundry
dishes piled up in the kitchen

everything but this
everything but hearing one more time
brain tumor unit

brain tumor unit
i call again
wait
on the line
who cares what else can i do

brain tumor unit
i leave another message
let's see if this is the one

i swallow my fear   invent   some strength

again
i start again

El cerebro no duele

hoy amanecí
imaginándome un dolor

una punzada
justo al lado izquierdo

donde dicen   que tengo el corazón

pero el cerebro no duele

porque es justamente
el que procesa   el dolor:

lo transmite   lo codifica   lo distribuye   (aunque no para sí
    mismo)
los músculos no eligen dormirse

a veces sin razón se paralizan dejan de sentir
y al despertarse explota todo acumulado:

de repente
son miles

de agujas desatadas clavándose al tiempo

el cerebro
en cambio

escoge cuándo
descansar

The Brain Feels No Pain

i woke up today
imagining a singular pain

a twinge
just there on the left side

where they say   i have my heart

but the brain doesn't hurt

because it is precisely
what processes   the pain:

transmits it   encodes it   distributes it   (but not for
   itself)
muscles do not choose to go to sleep

sometimes they become paralyzed for no reason at all stop feeling
and when they wake everything accumulated explodes:

suddenly
there are thousands

of unfettered needles pricking all at once

the brain
in contrast

chooses when
to rest

decide

dormir
olvidar

tomarse un respiro   al fin

apagarse

para soñar
que esto no está pasando
que fue una pesadilla

hasta que

una punzada
me despierta:

debe ser
que así duele la conciencia

decides

to sleep
to forget

to take a break   at last

to turn off

to dream
that this is not happening
that this was a nightmare

until

a twinge
wakes me:

it must be
that this is how consciousness hurts

II
Nombrar una herida en las palabras

II

TO NAME A WOUND INSIDE MY WORDS

Nombrar una herida en las palabras

I

there's a chance
that you might lose

your words

me dice el médico
después de mucho   interrogarlo

(porque prefiero   saber
quiero

entender
los riesgos   aunque sean   remotos   o lejanos)

en principio
vas a estar bien

no tienes por qué   angustiarte vas a recuperarte   completamente

aunque claro:
nunca se sabe del todo

primero está

lo impredecible
(pienso en la muerte
será eso y no lo dice   maría
no pienses en la muerte)

To Name a Wound Inside My Words

I

there's a chance
that you might lose

your words

the doctor tells me
after a lot of   questioning

(because i would rather   know
i want

to understand
the risks   even if they are   remote   or distant)

in principle
you'll be fine

there's no need   to worry you will recover   completely

but of course:
you never quite know everything

first there is

the unpredictable
(i think of death
it will be that and he doesn't say it   maría
don't think about death)

II

y luego

mis palabras

nunca pensé que estuvieran
en peligro

que algún día pudiera
no encontrarlas

siempre las palabras

venían
a rescatarme

con ellas cubría el dolor
bajo ellas me escondía

yo
que he sido mi voz

my words
doctor?
that would be the end
of me le digo

porque me podía doler el cuerpo
me podía doler la vida

podía tener el corazón y los huesos rotos

hasta perder

II

and then

my words

i never thought they would be
in danger

that someday i might
not find them

my words always

came
to my rescue

i covered my pain with them
beneath them i hid

i
who have been my voice

my words
doctor?
that would be the end
of me i tell him

because my body could ache
my life could hurt

my heart and bones broken

even lose

la cuenta de los golpes

pero tenía las palabras

para aferrarme a ellas
para decir voy a estar bien
para nombrar las heridas

para que al nombrarlas   comenzaran a sanar

count of the blows

but i had my words

could hold onto them
could say i'm going to be fine
could name each of my wounds

so that by naming them   they would begin to heal

III

¿con qué nombrar

una herida en las palabras?
¿cómo hacer para cerrarla?

¿cómo se vería

la cicatriz de mi silencio
o de mis palabras

rotas   caídas   extraviadas?

¿adónde iría a buscarlas si las pierdo?

¿cómo me encontraría?

¿con qué describiría
la forma   exacta

de esa

cicatriz?

¿sería una imagen?

III

with what to name

a wound inside my words?
what to do to close it?

how would the scar

of my silence look
or of my words

broken   fallen   missing?

where should i go to look for them if i lose them?

how could i find myself?

with what would i describe
the exact   shape

of that

scar?

would it be an image?

IV

veo todavía en la pantalla
esa imagen

del corazón dibujado en mi cerebro

no ha crecido nada
dice el médico   eso es buena señal

pero las cicatrices
tienden a encogerse

y la verdad
no sé qué es lo que tienes

no tengo idea probablemente
un tumor   pero sigo sin saber

por eso

me va a tocar
operarte   mejor

rápido
busquemos
una fecha   mejor pronto

IV

i still see that image
on the screen

of the heart drawn on my brain

it hasn't grown at all
the doctor says   that's a good sign

but scars
tend to shrink

and the truth is
i don't know what you have

i have no idea probably
a tumor   but i still don't know

that's why

i'll have to
operate   better

now
let's set
a date   the sooner the better

v

(vamos a actuar   por la incertidumbre

pienso
mientras habla

hay que saltar o saltar
cerrar los ojos porque él
no sabe nada

no saber nada no saber   pero saltar es menos peligroso

que

quedarme
quieta)

si llega a crecer después

sería
peor

la posibilidad   de sobrevivir
disminuye

bastante   no voy a mentirte
se riega muy rápido apenas acelera se expande te invade y no hay
    reversa
podrías necesitar quimioterapia

me van a abrir el cerebro para sacarme el corazón

v

(we should act now   because of the uncertainty

i think
while he speaks

we have to jump or jump
close my eyes because he
doesn't know anything

not knowing anything not knowing   but jumping is less dangerous

than

standing
still)

if it grows later

it would be
worse

the possibility   of survival
decreases

quite a lot   i'm not going to lie to you
it spreads very quickly as soon as it accelerates it expands invades
    you and there's no going back
you may need chemotherapy

they're going to open my brain to take out my heart

VI

¿voy a seguir siendo yo?
¿cómo-cómo quién voy a despertar?

tengo miedo
tengo tanto tanto miedo
que no sé dónde ponerlo
no hay espacio que lo contenga se desborda no hay lugar no hay
    lugar no hay refugio

no sé
con qué cubrirlo
se extiende y se extiende el territorio que abarca

tengo tanto tanto miedo

que no me cabe
en las palabras

no puedo empezar   a rodearlo

aunque tenga todavía
kilómetros y kilómetros de palabras y quiera extendérselas encima

no puedo empezar
a nombrarlo

ni siquiera ahora
que están todas
las palabras
conmigo

VI

am i still going to be me?
how-who will i wake up as?

i'm scared
i am so so scared
i don't know where to put so much fear
no space large enough to hold it all it overflows no place no place
    no shelter

i don't know
what to cover it with
the territory it crosses expands and expands

i have so much fear

so much fear doesn't fit
inside words

i can't begin   to go around it

even if i still have
kilometers and kilometers of words and i want to drape them over it

i can't begin
to name it

not even now
that all of them
the words
are with me

ni ahora

que están
todas
intactas

not even now

that they are
all of them
intact

Decir tengo miedo

y si lo mío es salvarme con palabras

tal vez decir

tengo miedo escribir tengo miedo en algo ayude

tengo miedo   y ya no sé

ya no distingo entre todos   los matices   del miedo

que me siguen
me agobian me entorpecen

tengo miedo de mí

tengo miedo de mi corazón roto
tengo miedo de que nunca se repare
de que se quede así quebrado para siempre

tengo miedo de mi corazón-cicatriz

tengo miedo de que sea   una herida abierta

tengo miedo de los médicos
de lo que vayan a encontrarme

tengo miedo de quedarme
aquí
estancada

To Say I Am Scared

and if my thing is to save myself with words

maybe to say

i'm scared to write i'm scared helps

i'm scared   and i no longer know

i can no longer distinguish between all   the nuances   of fear

that follow me
overwhelm me derail me

i'm scared of myself

i'm scared of my broken heart
i'm scared it will never heal
that it will stay broken like this forever

i'm scared of my heart-scar

i'm scared that it will be   an open wound

i'm scared of doctors
of what they're going to find inside me

i'm scared of staying
here
stuck

tengo miedo de ti

de no liberarme nunca
de que no te vayas

de que esta vez

pensar
no baste

de que las palabras
no sean
suficientemente materiales
para cubrir tu hueco

de que no sean tan hábiles
para cerrar heridas

de que mi cerebro
me traicione

tengo miedo de ser tan frágil

tengo miedo de ser
tan fuerte de lo triste
tan fuerte de lo rota

i'm scared of you

of never freeing myself
of you not leaving

that this time

thinking
isn't enough

that the words
are not
sufficient material
to fill your hollow

that they are not skillful enough
to close wounds

that my brain
betrays me

i'm scared of being so fragile

i'm scared of sadness
making me so strong
so strong from being broken

El lugar de las palabras

Para el doctor Javier Romero
que me encontró el lugar de las palabras

I

nunca había pensado
que las palabras   ocupan un espacio en el cerebro

un rincón preciso   justo irremplazable
hay un lugar en donde están almacenadas

tampoco había entendido
que todos los cerebros son distintos
que cada uno guarda el lenguaje donde puede

tú por ejemplo
dice el médico
lo debes tener en todas partes

vamos a buscar
exactamente

dónde aparece tu lenguaje dónde es que lo guardas
vamos a dar con el lugar de las palabras

para ver si está comprometido

el examen es una resonancia
(ya me han hecho tantas reconozco la cápsula cerrada y aún me
    aturden los ruidos)
pero esta vez vas a pensar palabras piénsalas no las digas en voz
    alta

The Place Where Words Reside

For Dr. Javier Romero
who found the place where words reside

I

i had never thought
that words   occupy a place in the brain

a precise corner   exact irreplaceable
there is a place where they are stored

i also hadn't understood
that all brains are different
that each one keeps language where it can

you for example
the doctor says
you must have yours everywhere

we're going to look
for the exact

place where your language appears where you keep it
let's find the place where words reside

to see if it is endangered

the test is an MRI
(i've already had so many i recognize the closed capsule and i'm
    still dazed by its noises)
but this time you're going to think words think them don't say
    them out loud

vas a ver en la pantalla una palabra por ejemplo bicicleta
y piensas bicicleta pedales timón cadena

para rastrear tu lenguaje
lo más importante
es la generación de verbos
ves por ejemplo la palabra puerta
y piensas todos los verbos que puedas mientras más mejor
pienso abrir cerrar derrumbar deshacer levantar empujar jalar
    portazo (no es un verbo pero es linda la palabra portazo
    concéntrate maría piensa un verbo)
door
open close that's about it
no olvides no mezclar los idiomas si ves la palabra en inglés
    piensa en inglés
mantenlos separados
vamos a hacerte un examen bilingüe
primero en español luego en inglés
you are going to see the first words in Spanish
en español se me ocurren más verbos
(puedo actuar con más ímpetu con más precisión
qué curioso que el lenguaje se mida con acciones
que hacer sea más fuerte que nombrar
yo pensaba que las palabras más palabras
eran los nombres de las cosas)
en todo caso el examen bilingüe
es porque tampoco sabía
que el cerebro guarda en un lugar la lengua materna
y en otro distinto los idiomas aprendidos
depende de la edad en que se aprendieron
(yo por ejemplo aprendí tarde y tengo acento en todos los
    idiomas)
el cerebro además procesa de manera diferente la información que
    sabe y la que no sabe

you will see a word on the screen for example bicycle
and you think bicycle pedals handlebars chain

to track your language
the most important thing
is verb generation
you see for example the word door
and you think as many verbs as you can the more the better
i think open close knock demolish unlatch lift push pull bang
    (it's not a verb but it's a nice word bang
    concentrate maría think of a verb)
door
open close that's about it
don't forget don't mix languages if you see the word in english
    think in english keep
them separate
we will give you a bilingual exam
first in spanish then in english
you are going to see the first words in spanish
i can think of more verbs in spanish
(i can act with greater impetus with more precision
how interesting that language is measured by actions
that doing is stronger than naming
i thought that words that are more words
were the names of things)
in any case the bilingual exam
is because i also didn't know
that the brain stores one's mother tongue in one place
and learned languages in a different one
where depends on when they were learned
(i for example was a late learner and have an accent in all
    languages)
the brain also processes what it knows differently from what it
    doesn't know

(yo por ejemplo no sé cuántos jugadores tiene un equipo de
    basketball: no sé en español
no sé en inglés y quieren que responda que piense algo que
    piense
ahora la respuesta
pienso entonces   cualquier número
supongo que no me estarán midiendo lo que sepa de deportes
    porque la verdad es que
no sé nada así que al menos en eso estoy tranquila: ahí no hay
    nada que perder)

quieren encontrar todas mis palabras
incluso las que uso para traducirme en esta tierra helada
can I think in Spanish?
le pregunto a la enfermera
me dice que sí afortunadamente
primero porque en inglés no conozco
el vocabulario específico de las bicicletas
ni sé nombrar las partes de una puerta
y sobre todo porque si hay que escoger
me quedo con mis palabras en español
de eso no cabe duda
prefiero salvarlas mil veces

(i for example don't know how many players are on a *basketball*
 team: i don't know
in spanish i don't know in english and they want me to answer to
 think
something to think of the answer now
so i think   any number
i guess they're not measuring what i know about sports because
 the truth is that i
don't know anything so at least i'm calm about that: there's
 nothing to lose there)

they want to find all my words
even the ones i use to translate myself in this frozen land
can i think in spanish?
i ask the nurse
she says yes fortunately
first because i don't know the specific bicycle
vocabulary in english
i can't even name the parts of a door
and above all if i have to choose
i'll keep my words in spanish
there's no doubt about that
i'd rather save them a thousand times over

II

por alguna razón
siempre pensé que las palabras
sólo sufrían de amenazas metafóricas

a diferencia del cuerpo o incluso el corazón
(porque ambos empezaban a romperse con el mundo)
y los oía quebrarse
sentía los huesos rotos
sentía la vida hecha polvo se anunciaba el dolor desde antes
cuando oía el golpe el estruendo el portazo la caída
por ejemplo
cuando llegaste tú

las palabras eran otra cosa
las palabras eran mías
y si se rompían yo podía repararlas

por ejemplo cuando no sabía
cómo nombrar la herida que dejaste
para empezar a cerrarla

escribí y escribí y escribí
tantos poemas
que no se parecían a tu nombre
que no eran suficientes
que no trazaban la forma de tu hueco

palabras y palabras y palabras que no bastaban para borrarte
pero ocupaban un espacio en la página
y al verlas dibujadas
comenzaba a sanar

II

for some reason
i always thought that words
only suffered from metaphorical threats

unlike the body or even the heart
(because both were starting to be broken by the world)
and i heard them breaking
i felt my broken bones
i felt my life shattered the pain was there before
when i heard the thump the boom the bang the fall
for example
when you arrived

the words were something else
the words were mine
and if they broke i could fix them

for example when i didn't know
how to name the wound you left behind
to begin to close it

i wrote and i wrote and i wrote
so many poems
they didn't look like your name
they weren't enough
they didn't trace the form of the hollow you left

words and words and words that weren't enough to erase you
but they took up space on the page
and seeing them drawn there
i started to heal

al rodearte con ellas
empezaba a convertirte en cicatriz

by surrounding you with them
i started to turn you into a scar

III

en cambio ahora
hay una bomba de tiempo en mi cerebro
que quién sabe cuándo explota
quién sabe cuándo se transforma
puede ser nunca o mañana o en un año

quién sabe
cuándo
empieza
a crecer

y a invadir
el territorio
donde viven
mis palabras

a desplazarlas
a acorralarlas
a doblegarlas
a arrinconarlas

¿dónde las voy a poner
si están comprometidas?

¿existirá algún lugar en donde pueda guardarlas?

¿cómo las protejo
cómo las escondo?

¿en dónde me resguardo
si he perdido mi refugio?

¿dónde vivo yo si las palabras son mi casa?

III

but now
there's a time bomb in my brain
and who knows when it will explode
who knows when it changes
it might be never or tomorrow or in a year

who knows
when
it begins
to grow

and invade
the territory
where my words
live

displace them
corral them
bend them
corner them

where am i going to put them
if they are endangered?

is there a place i can store them?

how do i protect them
how do i hide them?

where do i take shelter
if i have lost my refuge?

where do i live if words are my home?

A un centímetro

Para Maria Gatti
cuya cercanía cambia todo
y tantas veces me ha salvado por tanto

dicen que tengo
las palabras
a un centímetro

no hay nada del lenguaje en el tumor
no está comprometido

el lugar más cercano
en donde vimos algo
es a un centímetro

un centímetro es mucho en el cerebro
dice el médico
imagínate un kilómetro
imagínate una distancia larga
con la precisión de los aparatos es lejísimos

me imagino un centímetro

me imagino una regla
de esas que usaba para dibujar cuando era niña
me imagino la distancia que hay del uno al dos
diez milímetros

más o menos la longitud
de las huellas digitales en mi índice derecho

Within One Centimeter

For Maria Gatti
whose closeness changes everything
and has so many times saved me by so much

they say
my words
are one centimeter away

there is no trace of language in the tumor
it is not endangered

the closest place
where we saw something
is one centimeter away

one centimeter is a lot in the brain
the doctor says
imagine a kilometer
imagine a great distance
with the accuracy of these devices it is far away

i imagine one centimeter

i imagine a ruler
like those i used to draw when i was a little girl
i imagine the distance between the one and two
ten millimeters

about the longitude
of my right index fingerprint

me imagino que las palabras son mis huellas digitales
y lo que sea que esté a un centímetro
es también mi voz
(¿qué parte de mi voz?
¿qué tono perdería?)

porque yo toco este mundo con palabras
porque en las palabras estoy yo

¿o no?
¿no soy yo?

es algo a un centímetro que puede inflamarse

como vamos a cortar ese pedazo
el cerebro va a quedar inflamado
y puede que se inflame también
esa área a un centímetro

puede que pierdas las palabras por un tiempo
pero las recuperas
apenas pase la inflamación
te vamos a tratar con antiinflamatorios

me van a rescatar del silencio con antiinflamatorios

no tendría que haber daños permanentes
la operación no debería dejar secuelas

¿voy a volver a ser yo?
¿voy a poder despertarme?

tal vez yo con una palabra más
por no decir una palabra menos

i imagine that words are my fingerprints
and whatever is within one centimeter
is also my voice
(what part of my voice?
what tone would i lose?)

because i touch this world with words
because i am inside words

or am i?
isn't it me?

it is something that can become inflamed within one centimeter

since we're going to cut that piece out
your brain will become inflamed
and it's also possible there may be swelling
in that area within one centimeter

you may lose your words for a while
but you will get them back
as soon as the inflammation passes
we're going to treat you with anti-inflammatory drugs

i will be rescued from silence by anti-inflammatory drugs

there should be no permanent damage
the operation should leave no long-term effects

will i be me again?
will i be able to wake up?

maybe i will be me but with one more word
to not say one word less

sin duda una nueva cicatriz

o yo más frágil
o más fuerte de lo frágil

de saber que me salvé
por un centímetro

no doubt a new scar

or i'll be more fragile
or stronger from being fragile

knowing that i was saved
by one centimeter

III

Lo que pase cuando corten mi materia

III

WHAT WILL HAPPEN WHEN MY MATTER IS CUT AWAY

Una cicatriz

I

tengo cicatrices en el cuerpo

en la rodilla
en el tobillo
en las manos
en las piernas

cada cicatriz con su forma irrepetible
cada cicatriz una caída

tengo cicatrices en la vida
que ha sabido quebrarme tantas veces
quebrarme sin tregua quebrarme tan fuerte
tantas maneras de dejarme rota

tengo cicatrices en la vida
y no sé cuál es la piel que ha sanado
de qué está hecha
cómo es que me cubre
cuál es la materia
de esta piel alerta
para guardar derrumbes

dónde se acomodan
estas otras heridas
más grandes que las heridas
más profundas
cómo hacen para expandirse
qué espacio ocupan

A Scar

I

i have scars on my body

on my knee
on my ankle
on my hands
on my legs

each scar has its unrepeatable shape
each scar a fall

i have scars in my life
that has known how to break me so many times
break me without hesitating break me hard
so many ways to leave me broken

i have scars in my life
and i no longer know which skin has healed
what it is made of
how it can cover me
what is the material
of this alert skin
that holds in my landslides

where do these
other wounds belong
larger than my deepest
wounds
how do they expand
what space do they occupy

para empezar a cerrarse

no una caída de bicicleta
no una botella estallada en el pie

ni vidrio ni madera ni metal ni pavimento

de qué están hechas las heridas
cuántas veces me rompieron
cómo hice para curarme
y para tejer cicatrices

dónde quedó esa huella
si no puedo borrarla
dónde quedó marcada
si está siempre guiándome
si yo soy la silueta de esa herida
si camino a su paso

dónde quedó esa huella
que me hizo ser quien soy

cómo me cosí esa cicatriz

to begin to close

not a fall from a bicycle
not a broken bottle on my foot

not glass or wood or metal or pavement

what are wounds made of
how many times was i broken
what did i do to cure myself
and to mend scars

where did that trace go
if i can't erase it
where did it leave its mark
if it is always guiding me
if i am the silhouette of that wound
if i walk with it

where did that trace go
that made me who i am

how did i stitch up that scar

II

ahora algo sospecho
de repente algo entiendo algo intuyo

cuando me dicen los médicos perplejos

que
lo que tengo

podría ser
una cicatriz en el cerebro
una cicatriz

cómo me di ese golpe

me preguntan
para explicar
la imagen insólita
de una figura estampada en forma de corazón
cerca de la frente
pero adentro no en la piel
a través del cráneo
en el lóbulo frontal izquierdo para ser exacta

cuál es el golpe que pudo dejármela
cuántos golpes la formaron

pensar para salvarme
hirió más hondo
que el vidrio el metal el pavimento

pensar para amortiguar los golpes

II

now i suspect something
suddenly i understand something i intuit

when the perplexed doctors tell me

that
what i have

could be
a scar in my brain
a scar

how did i get that wound

they ask me
to explain
the unusual image
of a heart-shaped figure pressed
close to my forehead
but inside not on my skin
through my skull
on the left frontal lobe to be exact

what was the blow that could have left it
how many blows did it take to make it

to think to save myself
wounded more deeply
than the glass the metal the pavement

to think to cushion the blows

para lidiar conmigo

porque nací frágil

nací sintiendo todo tantas veces más
para lidiar conmigo

porque nací fuerte
nací lista para rearmarme para ensamblarme con cenizas
y comenzar de nuevo comenzar de cero de nada comenzar
    siempre   levantarme

to deal with me

because i was born fragile

i was born feeling everything so much more
to deal with me

because i was born strong
i was born to reassemble myself to assemble myself out of the ashes
and begin again begin from scratch from nothing
    always begin   to get up

III

pensar para salvarme de la pena
era una herida
que tenía que sanar en algún sitio
una huella del derrumbe
tenía que dibujarse

había que llorar ese dolor inmenso
había que llorarlo en algún lado
había que llorarlo con el cuerpo
porque pensar para
salvarme
se hizo herida

y ahora   cicatriz

ojalá sea solamente eso
una cicatriz
que vean una cicatriz cuando me abran
no un tumor no una sentencia de muerte

una cicatriz
una marca de haber sobrevivido

III

to think to save myself from sorrow
was a wound
that had to heal somewhere
a trace of the collapse
had to draw itself

that immense pain had to be mourned
it had to be mourned somewhere
it had to be mourned with the body
because to think to
save myself
became itself a wound

and now   a scar

i hope it's only that
a scar
that they see a scar when they open me
not a tumor not a death sentence

a scar
a mark of having survived

Para un cuerpo que está solo

I

porque mi cuerpo está solo
tendré que rodearlo

abrazarme las rodillas
recogerme el pelo
preparar mi cabeza para que la abran

porque con mi cerebro estoy sola

estoy sola con mis manos
estoy sola con mi miedo
estoy sola con mi espalda

estoy sola
con estas punzadas de dolor
que ya no sé si invento

ya no sé si me duele la conciencia
pero las siento tan agudas como agujas
atravesándome mil veces

¿me irán a abrir con una aguja?

For a Body That Is Alone

I

because my body is alone
i'll have to surround it

hug my knees
gather up my hair
prepare my head to be opened

because i am alone with my brain

i am alone with my hands
i am alone with my fear
i am alone with my back

i am alone
with this throbbing pain
i no longer know if i am inventing

i no longer know if my conscience hurts
but it feels as sharp as needles
piercing me a thousand times

are they going to cut me open with a needle?

II

tantas veces era yo contra mi cuerpo:

yo luchando
porque me dijeron que no era suficiente
entonces creí que era mi cuerpo
el que impedía que me amaran

quería ocupar menos espacio
quería ser menos rara
quería una cara de esas
en las que cualquiera se siente en casa

ahora mi cuerpo es mi casa

y tengo miedo de cuando me corten
para poder abrirme el cráneo
este pelo crespo
del que tanto renegué
porque me dijeron que tenía mucho volumen como yo
y había que aplacarlo para que me amaran

tengo miedo de que me duela
esta piel oscura
por la que de niña me excluyeron

tengo miedo de no volver
a abrir los ojos
con los que tanto me miraba al espejo
buscándome defectos:

tienes la nariz muy ancha

II

so many times it was me against my body:

me fighting
because they told me i wasn't good enough
so i thought it was my body
that kept me from being loved

i wanted to take up less space
i wanted to be less strange
i wanted one of those faces
where anyone feels at home

now my body is my home

and i'm afraid of when they cut
so they can crack my skull open
this curly hair
i tried so hard to disown
because i was told it took up a lot of space like me
and i had to tame it to be loved

i'm afraid this dark skin
the reason they excluded me as a girl
will hurt

i'm afraid i won't again
open those eyes
i used so much to look at myself in the mirror
looking for my flaws:

your nose is too wide

las cejas muy gruesas
tienes amplias las caderas
no te cabe la ropa

your eyebrows are too thick
you have ample hips
you don't fit in these clothes

III

ahora nada en mí es demasiado

ahora quiero ocupar todo ese espacio
en el que antes intentaba encogerme
para que al fin me vieran

ahora quiero expandirme
estar en donde estoy
llenar todos mis rincones

ahora quiero estar aquí
sin cambiarme nada

porque estoy sola conmigo
y eso es suficiente

por todo lo que amo
a este cuerpo que está solo

III

now nothing in me is too much

now i want to occupy all that space
i used to try to shrink myself into
so that i could finally be seen

now i want to expand
be where i am
fill all my corners

now i want to be here
without changing a thing

because i am alone with myself
and that is enough

for all that i love
this body that is alone

Tengo miedo del túnel

tengo miedo del túnel
tengo miedo de cuando me digan cuenta hasta diez respira piensa algo bonito

y me voy a ir durmiendo

y durante cinco horas me van a abrir el cráneo
y ni cómo saber qué es lo que van a encontrar
si hay en mi cerebro una bomba de tiempo

o si sólo nací con el corazón en la cabeza
(eso explicaría tantas cosas)

tengo miedo del túnel
tengo miedo de estar abierta en una sala de cirugía
tengo miedo de que me examinen
el cerebro desde adentro

tengo miedo de la materia
tengo miedo de la materia gris
de que algo esté dañado

tengo miedo de la materia que soy
tengo miedo de que la corten
tengo miedo de lo que pase

cuando corten mi materia

I Am Scared Of The Tunnel

i am scared of the tunnel
i am scared of when they tell me to count to ten breathe think of
    something beautiful

and i'm going to start to fall asleep

and for five hours my skull is going to be cracked open
and there's no way to know what they will find
if there's a time bomb in my brain

or if i was only born with my heart in my head
(this would explain so many things)

i am scared of the tunnel
i am scared of being open in an operating room
i am scared of them examining
my brain from the inside

i am scared of the matter
i am scared of the gray matter
that something is damaged

i am scared of the matter that i am
i am scared they will cut it
i am scared of what will happen

when they cut away my matter

IV

Cómo me cosí esa cicatriz

IV

How I Stitched Up That Scar

Ese sonido

For Dr. William Curry
who saved my life

es el sonido de la piel cerrándose supongo
la cicatriz cosiéndose
los diecinueve puntos de metal

o tal vez algo más profundo
algo que craquea desde los huesos

las placas tectónicas de mi cráneo

juntándose otra vez
después del terremoto
reacomodándose

o tal vez algo más profundo aún

tal vez es mi cerebro lidiando con su hueco
haciendo su duelo

echando de menos el corazón que le quitaron

buscando a toda costa una materia
para cubrir la ausencia

creando
como puede
conexiones

de la nada

That Sound

For Dr. William Curry
who saved my life

it's the sound of skin closing i suppose
the scar stitching itself
the nineteen metal stitches

or perhaps something deeper
something that crackles up from the bones

the tectonic plates of my skull

coming together again
after the earthquake
rearranging themselves

or perhaps something even deeper

maybe it's my brain grappling with its hollow
grieving

missing the heart that was removed

searching desperately for some material
to conceal the absence

creating
as it can
connections

out of nothing

conexiones
nuevas
para el vacío

tapándolo con algo

tal vez
ese sonido

es mi cerebro
reinventándose

new
connections
for the void

covering it with something

perhaps
that sound

is my brain
reinventing itself

Un examen de rutina

apégate a los hechos:

el papelito donde anotaste tu número de paciente 5948345

no sueltes la precisión
aprieta en el puño la certeza
de esas siete cifras que van a amarrarte a la muñeca
para saber quién eres
cuando te hayas quitado la ropa
y hasta el esmalte de las uñas para que puedan conectarte

medical record number
date of birth

aférrate a los detalles:

escoge la sudadera
con cuidado
aunque sea irrelevante
porque te van a hacer ponerte
la bata de hospital

cúbrete la cicatriz de la cabeza

con una pañoleta que puedas desatar
quítate las gafas
aunque veas todo borroso y no distingas ni siquiera
las caras de las enfermeras apurándose por los pasillos
(igual vas a cerrar los ojos)
no te pongas flores en el pelo ni lleves joyas
porque no hay dónde guardarlas

A Routine Examination

stick to the facts:

the piece of paper where you wrote down your patient number 5948345

don't let go of this precision
clench in your fist the certainty
of those seven figures they are going to wrap around your wrist
to know who you are
when you have removed your clothes
and even your nail polish so they can hook you up

medical record number
date of birth

stick to the details:

pick out your sweatshirt
carefully
even if it's irrelevant
because they're going to make you put on
the hospital gown

cover the scar on your head

with a scarf you can untie
take off your glasses
even if everything is blurry and you can't make out
the faces of the nurses rushing through the corridors
(you're still going to close your eyes)
don't wear flowers in your hair or wear jewelry
because there's nowhere to keep it

(y en medio de la angustia
tampoco
hay nada que adornar)

repite
lo que vas a responder a las preguntas de rutina
cuando tengas que llenar los formularios

do you have a personal history of cancer?
yes
(pero aún no tengo palabras para contarla)
(tengo escritas las palabras de los médicos y a veces les doy vueltas
    como un loro:
astrocitoma de segundo grado astrocitoma de   las mías
    en cambio se me escapan)

repasa cómo decir en inglés
hace seis meses me operaron
    del cerebro

quédate con los hechos no les digas
I hope it doesn't come back
I'm really scared of needles

cierra los ojos y aprieta el puño
cuando vayan a chuzarte

quédate con tu miedo
cuando entres a la cápsula

medical record number
date of birth

podrías repetir poemas

(and in all this anguish
there's
nothing to adorn)

repeat
how you're going to respond to the routine questions
when you have to fill out the forms

do you have a personal history of cancer?
yes
(but i don't yet have the words to explain it)
(i have written down the words the doctors use and sometimes i parrot them:
second degree astrocytoma astrocytoma of   but mine escape me)

review how to say in English
hace seis meses me operaron del cerebro   six months ago
    i had brain surgery

stick with the facts and don't tell them
i hope it doesn't come back
i'm really scared of needles

close your eyes and make a fist
when they are going to prick you

hold onto your fear
when you enter the closed capsule

medical record number
date of birth

you could recite poems

para ahuyentar la soledad
para pensar en otra cosa
en esa cámara cerrada
para cubrir con algo
los ruidos que te aturden

¿aparecerán en la imagen los versos dibujados en mi cerebro?

¿o interrumpidos
quebrados por esa voz que en mí repite
maría tengo miedo
por qué a mí
por qué   este desamparo
y cómo apagar tantas preguntas?

mejor
responde a lo concreto:

can you lay still for 45 minutes?
yes

do you have metal in your body?
no
(pero sí tengo un cuerpo frágil
ojalá no vuelvan a abrirlo)

are you claustrophobic?
no
(pero le temo a la muerte como todos
tal vez
sí soy claustrofóbica aquí en el encierro de esta incertidumbre)

siempre hay posibilidad de recurrencia
puede ser mañana

to dispel your loneliness
to think about something else
in that closed chamber
to cover the noises
that stun you with something

will the lines i see in my head appear in the image?

or interrupted
cracked by that voice inside me that repeats
maría tengo miedo   i am scared
why me
why this helplessness   este desamparo
how do i turn off so many questions?

better
respond to the concrete:

can you lay still for 45 minutes?
yes

do you have metal in your body?
no
(but i do have a fragile body
i hope they don't open it again)

are you claustrophobic?
no
(but i fear death like everyone else
maybe
yes i am claustrophobic here in the confinement of this uncertainty)

there is always a possibility of a recurrence
it could be tomorrow

*o nunca o en diez o veinte años
no voy a poder decirte
que te curaste del todo
que te olvides de esto
algún día
podrías necesitar radioterapia o una nueva operación
un cáncer antes de los treinta años es rarísimo
vamos a tener que examinarte muchas veces por mucho tiempo*

resultado:

*positivo
una mutación patogénica fue detectada en el gen TP53*

*no fue por azar
naciste predispuesta
tal vez eso lo explique*

yo

que tanto necesito explicaciones
trato de quedarme en lo concreto

ese también es un hecho
(nací como nací)

pero no sé cómo rodearlo cómo nombrarlo dónde acomodarlo
entonces a qué me aferro:

*medical record number
date of birth*

or never or in ten or twenty years
i won't be able to tell you
that you are fully cured
that you can forget about this
someday
you might need radiation therapy or another operation
cancer before the age of thirty is extremely rare
we're going to have to run tests on you for a long time

results:

positive
a pathogenic mutation was detected in the TP53 gene

it wasn't by chance
you were born predisposed
maybe that explains it

i

so in need of explanations
try to remain in the concrete

that is also a fact
(i was born as i was)

but i don't know how to surround it how to name it where to place it
so what am i clinging to:

medical record number
date of birth

Escóndete en tu abrigo

I

esa cicatriz

va
a dolerte
con el frío

me habían advertido   antes

y yo había borrado la advertencia
porque ya me salió otra vez el pelo

aunque todavía
me amarre pañoletas de colores
por costumbre por si acaso

Hide Inside Your Coat

I

that scar

is going
to hurt
in cold weather

they had warned me   before

and i had forgotten the warning
because my hair has already grown back

although i still
use colorful scarves
out of habit just in case

II

no recordaba
lo del frío
hasta ahora

hasta hoy cuando el invierno
cae

sin aviso
y esta punzada en el cráneo me dice

que estoy aquí

que estuve a punto
de no estar

que tuve la cabeza

abierta
cinco horas
en una sala de cirugía

que casi pierdo las palabras

II

i didn't remember
the thing about the cold
until now

until today when winter
falls

without warning
and this sharp pain in my skull tells me

that i am here

that i was about to
not be

that my head was

open
for five hours
in an operating room

that i almost lost my words

III

cuando empieza
a colarse
        este frío
tan debajo de la piel

recuerdo que soy frágil

III

when   this cold
starts to
creep under
my skin

i remember i am fragile

IV

saco el abrigo

hecho para un invierno canadiense
aunque apenas comienza noviembre

(en febrero
        ya
                me veo perdida

sin
        bajo qué
                refugiarme)

IV

i take out my coat

made for a canadian winter
although november is just beginning

(in february
                i already
                              see myself lost

without
        something
                to shelter me)

v

no hay
    gorros
    ni orejeras
que puedan
    cubrirme de

esa

punzada elocuente

que me deja muda
y mi cerebro me habla

v

there are no
                stocking caps
                or earmuffs
that can
                protect me from

that

eloquent stabbing pain

that leaves me speechless
and my brain speaks to me

VI

me dice maría
casi nos perdemos
casi nos apagan

me dice maría
somos frágiles

VI

maría it tells me
we almost got lost
they almost shut us down

maría it tells me
we are fragile

VII

pero

sobre todo cuando vengan a quebrarte
hazte la fuerte

cuando te rompan baila hazte la fuerte

maría
escóndete en tu abrigo

VII

but

especially when they come to crack you open
pretend to be strong

when they break you dance pretend to be strong

maría
hide inside your coat

Palabras piel

> *palabras número palabras tiempo*
> *palabras piel*
> Rose Ausländer

si pudiera escoger otra piel

sería oscura como la mía
y estaría hecha de palabras

si pudiera decir *palabras-piel*

y así tener un cuerpo
como el mío

pero

elocuente
al quebrarse

si tuviera un cuerpo que dijera
por ejemplo *aquí estoy no me he ido* por ejemplo *sobrevivo*

un cuerpo que diera razones y porqués
y no este aturdimiento este cansancio estos huesos casi polvo de
    tantas veces rotos

cuánto entendería   entonces:

si tuviera palabras
en vez de cicatrices

Skin Words

> *number words time words*
> *skin words*
> Rose Ausländer

if i could pick another skin

it would be dark like mine
and it would be made of words

if i could say *skin-words*

and that way have a body
like mine

but

eloquent
when cracked

if i had a body that said
for example *here i am i haven't left* for example *i survive*

a body that would give reasons and whys
and not this bewilderment this weariness these bones almost dust
    from so much breaking

how much i would understand   then:

if i had words
instead of scars

Frida Kahlo

I

si pudiera pintar como frida kahlo
tendría muchos bocetos para los huesos rotos

primero a lápiz
luego iría agregando
los colores

ensayaría siluetas
volvería a empezar
cruzaría líneas y contornos

hasta dar
con la forma exacta de la herida

entonces
        probaría

todas las distintas
tonalidades del rojo
para el cuerpo ensangrentado

hasta encontrar
ese matiz justo de lo frágil

Frida Kahlo

I

if i could paint like frida kahlo
i'd have a lot of sketches of my broken bones

first in pencil
then i'd continue adding
colors

i would try out silhouettes
i would start again
i would make hatch marks and contours

until i found
the exact shape of my wound

then
       i would try

each of the different
shades of red
for the body bleeding

until i find
the right nuance of fragility

II

la expresión de su dolor
está en la imagen:

los ojos entrecerrados
la boca resignada que no grita
apenas se abre
tal vez murmura un gemido

las palabras
en el título del cuadro
inscritas en el letrero sostenido por palomas
UNOS CUANTOS PIQUETITOS!
así en mayúscula
exclamando

contienen
       la ironía

porque ella
en la imagen

desnuda
herida

todavía con un zapato puesto
el de su pierna izquierda rota
todavía con el tacón

que disimulaba
su pierna más corta que la otra

II

the expression of her pain
is in the image:

her half-closed eyes
her resigned mouth that doesn't scream
that hardly opens
maybe she murmurs a groan

the words
in the title of the painting
inscribed on the placard held up by pigeons
A FEW SMALL PECKS!
in capital letters
exclaim

contain
       the irony

because she
in the image

naked
wounded

still wearing one shoe
the one on her broken left leg
still with the heel

that concealed
one leg was shorter than the other

(uno de sus tantos desbalances)

ella no puede decir
UNOS CUANTOS PIQUETITOS!

(one of her many imbalances)

she cannot say
A FEW SMALL PECKS!

III

a las palabras
en cambio
les cabe la ironía

de un cuerpo quebrado
que aún sabe nombrarse

de un dolor ciego
que es clarividente

para ver
lo absurdo y lo pequeño

III

the words
in contrast
hold room for the irony

of a broken body
that can still name itself

of a blind pain
that is clairvoyant

to see
the absurd and the small

IV

esa voz está en el cuerpo
y fuera de él
esa voz es y no es las heridas

es la perspectiva
imposible

a la vez desde arriba
y desde muy adentro

alguien que observa desde el techo el cuerpo roto y piensa
    pobrecita
alguien que está también muy al fondo de ese cuerpo *unos cuantos*
    piquetitos

IV

that voice is in the body
and outside of it
that voice is and is not the wounds

it is the impossible
perspective

both from above
and from deep inside

someone looking down from the ceiling at the broken body and
    thinks
poor thing someone who is also deep inside that body *a few small
    pecks*

v

pero yo no puedo pintar como frida

no tengo su paleta de colores
no tengo la precisión
de cada corte en la piel

no tengo una cama sencilla en medio de un cuarto
en donde una mujer adolorida

se retuerce
serena
sopesando su dolor

v

but i can't paint like frida

i don't have her color palette
i don't have the precision
of each cut on the skin

i don't have a single bed in the middle of a room
where an aching woman

writhes
serenely
pondering her pain

VI

sólo me queda la voz

me queda la voz frágil quebrada
que no puede pintar de rojo sus heridas

me queda la voz sin forma sin imágenes
que no puede dibujar las grietas que se abren
en sus huesos al romperse

me queda la voz sola   desprovista

sin distancia

sin más remedio
que ser al tiempo

su dolor
y su ironía

VI

only my voice is left

only my fragile broken voice
that cannot paint its wounds red

i am left with a formless voice a voice without images
that cannot draw the cracks opening up
in her bones as they break

my voice is left alone   devoid

without distance

with no other choice
but to be at the same time

its pain
and its irony

Translator's Note

In the summer of 2025, I read an interview with the Argentine poet María Negroni in the Spanish newspaper *ABC*. In talking about the complex and often dichotomous role of language, in particular for writers, Negroni recalled lines from poems by two poets instrumental in her formation:

The Spanish poet Aníbal Núñez writes, "para ser río, al río le sobra el nombre" ["to be a river, calling it river isn't necessary"], indicating that the river *is*, only *is*. It doesn't need words. And when you name the river, you're supplanting it. You are left with the word river. And then there's the Argentine poet Alejandra Pizarnik who asked, "if I say water will I drink?/ if I say bread will I eat?" There is always a divorce between the word and the world. The word helps you get closer and, at the same time, it distances you from it.

Negroni's attention to the limits of linguistic expression in Núñez and Pizarnik sparked my own revelation about a fundamental attribute of the book *The Place Where Words Reside* by the Colombian poet María Gómez Lara. For Gómez Lara, the verbal utterance "is life, is breath, is repair"; words are essential for her, for her own psychological and emotional healing, and perhaps even corporeal healing.

The week before, I'd spent a day with Gómez Lara, discussing my translation of her book. Our conversations touched upon the numerous challenges that often arise when guiding poems from one language to another, such as how to convey the musicality behind her use of medical terminology or the intensifying tension simmering under the surface of those personal anecdotes laden with layered references about her past, about her tendency toward solitude, about race that are then woven through the text. But we also explored the lexical nuances that are repeated throughout the book, working together to hone those areas emanating emotional ripples inside words like "fear, like being frightened, being afraid, being scared". We searched for roots, for traces of concepts inside the Spanish that could be revealed in these English versions. In her poems, repetitions are not redundant but ongoing dialogues between her illogical and emotional self which is unable to comprehend the news she has just received from her oncologist, and her rational and practical self, which balances this information with the reality that she needs to continue to teach and take her coursework and live her life. Words for Gómez Lara are not only signs imposed upon objects and emotions, but they are like air, that necessary complexity of elements needed for her existence.

In 2017, María Gómez Lara had a brain tumor removed which was dangerously close to the place where language resides in the brain. *The Place Where Words Reside* is about that experience—about the physical and emotional terror the body feels after a medical diagnosis and through treatment, but also about her vital relationship to language itself, the expression of the symbiotic bond between the physical and linguistic. In an early poem, Gómez Lara writes: "your thing was to save yourself with words." Then she forces herself to speak, to "tell your brain   repeat it repeat it/ please don't get sick." Here, language is a fragile body, fragile because it too can become inflamed and infirmed, because it can break. And also because language is its own curative.

Gómez Lara's language is smooth, liquid, cascading in Spanish, and my challenge was how to carry that music and other aspects of her intricate poetics into English. In some cases, she gives a simple account of what happens or will transpire in the operating room. She attempts to comprehend what is happening in her brain, in that "heart-shaped spot," and what will happen after the swollen brain tissue relaxes and the anesthesia dissipates. And in other poems she searches for the cause of the tumor, wondering if illness comes from solitude, skin color, hair texture, wonders if it can be controlled, if she could have done something else. But this book does not dwell in the experience of illness alone. Instead, Gómez Lara explores her physical and emotional transformation. Emotional signifiers like "fear, afraid, scared", when spoken, influence how the body feels and reacts. The poet fears for her words, both their power upon her body, but also fears losing access to them. To lose the words would be as if she were losing her own life. She is scared and scarred and, yet, not willing to let either feeling silence her.

"Truth is also invented," writes Antonio Machado. Gómez Lara takes a painful personal truth away from the sphere of private medical reports and into the realm of shared truth, shared need. When her pain becomes more than itself, when it becomes theme, literature is born. Moving and brilliant, *The Place Where Words Reside* offers an overwhelming, profound, and unabashed sincerity. María Gómez Lara is one of the rare poets who can mend the distance between word and world, who has endured the cold solitude of an operating room, of an uncertain recovery and made poetry from this experience, poetry that recognizes that words "hold room for the irony/ of a broken body/ that can still name itself/ of a blind pain/ that is clairvoyant/ to see/ the absurd and the small." Her voice remains, however, and it is our fortune to have access to it through these poems.

www.ingramcontent.com/pod-product-compliance
Lightning Source LLC
Chambersburg PA
CBHW040031180426
43196CB00047B/2947